Passages
Life's Journey

BETTY JANE'S D·I·A·R·Y

Passages

Life's Journey

PERSONAL THOUGHTS & REFLECTIONS

BETTY JANE WYLIE

HarperCollins*Publishers*Ltd

Design by Styles Design Inc.

First Edition

Canadian Cataloguing in Publication Data

Wylie, Betty Jane, 1931—
Passages: life's journey

ISBN 0-00-215686-5

1. Life change events. I. Title.

BF637.L53W9 1991   155.9   C91-094734-1

91 92 93 94 95 T-S 5 4 3 2 1

To Peter Flemington

Acknowledgements

*B*etty Jane's Diary was originally written for a radio series produced and distributed by Berkeley Studio, Toronto. I'd like to thank Peter Flemington for his insights and assistance during those four years, and Nancy Colbert, both for her loyalty and for her perception of me and my audience.

You're Only as Old as You Feel

We live in a society and a century that prizes youth. To be young is to have it all. To be young is to be beautiful. George Bernard Shaw once said, with some envy, "Youth is wasted on the young," but he recognized thereby the ruefulness of age.

There is a double standard of aging. Older women are treated as invisible. They are ignored—by cosmetic ads as well as by older men. Older men are not criticized if they date and marry sweet young things. Older women, and that means any woman over forty, are.

Few women have the nerve to tell their age, because the statistic alone classifies them and shuts them off from the courtesies and attentions shown to younger women. As for getting a job, it's called the RHW— retired housewife—syndrome, whereby a woman over forty finds it very tough to return to the work force, not merely because of a lack of skills but also for the simple fact of her age.

"You don't look forty," people said to the feminist writer Gloria Steinem. "This is what forty looks like," she replied, and she made it look great. Older women have to be frankly forty and tell people. We are not senile, we are not over the hill. We are still vital, energetic, attractive people, and we are not ready to be put away on a shelf of age. We owe it to ourselves and to younger women coming after us. Youth will join us soon enough. All it takes is time.

Wrinkle City I

$\mathcal{I}$n T.S. Eliot's play *The Family Reunion*, a character called Harry returns after many years to find his family almost unchanged. He exclaims in dismay, "You all look so wrinkled and so young!" And it is a terrible accusation.

I hope it doesn't happen to you and me.

Our society is so youth-oriented that people are afraid of wrinkles—though they never seem to quit smoking, which causes wrinkles, and they keep on lying in the sun, which causes wrinkles, and they worry a lot, which causes wrinkles.

What I want to know is, what's wrong with a few wrinkles? I wouldn't want to live a lifetime and not have something to show for it, including some life- and laugh-lines.

Our skin is on the outside, but why shouldn't it show some evidence of what has gone on *inside* us during our lives? That line about beauty being only skin-deep is nonsense. Beauty isn't in the skin at all, it's what's inside the package that counts. Honor and integrity, love and truthfulness—these are the inner qualities that contribute to beauty in a face, and they emerge only after a lot of years of living.

Think for a moment of a truly beautiful person that you know. I mean beautiful, not movie-star pretty. Decide for yourself whether wrinkles have anything to do with that beauty. They do, in the way I'm talking about; they don't, if your emphasis is on mere youthfulness.

Welcome to Wrinkle City!

Wrinkle City, Part II

The poet Coleridge once commented that there are three kinds of old ladies: "that dear old soul; that old woman; and that witch." He said almost all women could hope for was to be "that old woman," but that they could try to avoid being labeled "witches," (these days, read bitches). It's not easy, I'm sure, when your bones ache and you're lonely and your tea bag is getting weaker.

I save cartoons. I run a clipping service for my friends, in fact, and send them cartoons I think are appropriate. I mean, what are friends and fridge doors for? But I also keep cartoons for myself and tape them into my diary.

I have one I couldn't part with. It shows an old woman stitching viciously on a sampler. Behind her on the wall are others that she has finished. One says: THE FOOD IS TERRIBLE. Another reads: MY LEGS ARE KILLING ME. The third goes: THE CHILDREN DON'T CALL.

I guess that old woman was labeled a witch. But at least she's doing something about it, stitching her complaints into mottoes she can hang on the wall.

Age doesn't happen all at once, of course. It isn't like turning a corner and suddenly, there it is. It's a long time since you felt that you could have danced all night, but that doesn't say you can't still dance. The first signs of approaching age are gentle, and you recognize them ruefully but with no great panic. Plenty of time yet.

There is also plenty of time, while you are collecting your silver hairs and holding back the moment of truth with L'Oreal (women) or Grecian Formula (men), to decide what your wrinkles are going to look like. None of us can avoid worry-lines, but I think we have some say in whether or not we get frown-furrows or smile-crinkles. We all get the faces we deserve, said Nietzsche, and I think the face has a great deal to do with whether we get the label, too: "dear old soul," "that old woman," or "that witch."

Ugly is Only Skin Deep

A very lovely friend of mine recently had a face-lift. Face-lifts used to be mysterious operations undergone only by fading Hollywood movie actresses and aging European countesses, but since the public transformation of several prominent North American women, face-lifts have become acceptable, public and "in."

My friend has emphasized appearance all her life. She was a model and is now a consultant. So when her face started to droop, it was important to her to stem the tide, or hold back the dawn, or put her finger in the dike, or whatever.

My friend had a very delicate, very successful job done on her face and feels it was worth every penny of the exorbitant amount it cost her. She lives in another city but I saw her recently, my first viewing since her face job.

"What do you think?" she asked triumphantly. It was scarcely a question.

"You're lovely," I said. "You always were. But I see more happiness and confidence than you've had for a while."

How could I answer her accurately? I've known her since I was eight years old, and I see her spirit when I look at her. I see her with my heart's eye.

That's how God sees us, too. He looks past the lines and the sags and wrinkles and looks at our spirits, our true selves.

It's in 1 Samuel, 16:7. "Man looks at the outward appearance, but God looks at the heart."

It Wasn't a Good Likeness

We are told that part of liking ourselves is accepting ourselves as we are, with all our knobs and warts, even as God accepts us. I go along with that—up to a point. I have to tell you something that happened to me recently that changed my thinking somewhat.

I received a huge glossy photograph taken of me while I was giving a speech. The picture was mounted on a large cardboard mat emblazoned with the logo of the organization I had been addressing, and with a personal note from the president written across the bottom. Obviously, it was intended to be a permanent memento of my time on stage.

In the picture I am wearing a neck-mike, and my chin is tucked down triple to speak into it. My mouth is open, my hands are clasped but open wide, with the thumbs out—splayed, really. The cord of the mike snakes down my front into a power-pack purse tied around my waist. I look dreadful.

My older daughter said I looked like Shelley Winters doing her fat-mama number. All I knew was I hated the picture. "It's not me," I said. "Tear it up," said Liz. So I did.

What a freeing thing to do! I tore up a part of myself I didn't like and don't have to accept. I will continue to maintain the image for myself, as well as for others, of a person I can accept. See?—that's how my thinking has changed. You don't have to accept all of yourself. You can reject some parts you don't like. You can turn away from them, cut them out of your life. You can tear up a bad picture and go on, believing in a better image of you.

Growing Pains

*D*o kids still have growing pains? I can remember when I was a kid that it was a legitimate problem. No one scoffed at the name, unscientific as it was. Nowadays, I suppose the symptoms are attributed to a calcium deficiency and they are dealt with almost before they start.

I remember my growing pains. I had them the summer I was twelve, when I suddenly stopped being short and pudgy. I earned money that summer by running after two two-year-old cousins of mine. The boys were the main reason I lost weight. Hard enough to run after one two-year-old, but two, in two different directions—man, that's running! I had a growing pain as I was running one day, it was so bad that it stopped me in my tracks. I ended up on my hands and knees, crawling up the steps of my cousin's cottage to tell them the boys were loose.

We all keep having growing pains, as long as we live—if we're lucky. We don't regard it as good fortune at the time. Any change is painful, as growth is uncomfortable. We would all like life to stay on the plateau, then we'd never have to bother with another mountain. No more climbing, no more struggle—we sigh for it as we gird our loins for another assault.

And yet, we grow only by struggle, get stronger as we put forth an effort, change as we adapt. When are we ever going to be smart enough, knowing all that, to look pain and change right in the teeth and say, "Thank you, thank you for the opportunity to keep on growing"?

Old Shoe Time

My brother used to have a Fun Book that I loved. It was one of those huge fun-for-rainy-days books, and it had a wonderful assortment of solitary activities as well as family quizzes and mysteries. One of my favorite sections in the book was a series of time-sequence puzzles.

There was shown, for example, a series of pictures depicting the life of a pair of shoes—from their purchase, brand-new, through a lot of walking, getting gum stuck to one sole, breaking a lace and having it knotted, through rain, through snow, until finally the shoes were broken and run-down and old. But all the pictures were mixed up, and you had to figure out the correct order they should be in to tell the sequence of events correctly. I thought it was fascinating.

I often think of it when I look at people's faces. We change, all of us. We encounter rain and storms and broken promises and defeats and all kinds of things that break in our faces and wear us down. Time alone, the sequence of time, can use up a face.

I don't mind wrinkles, don't misunderstand me. Was it Shaw who said that every wrinkle stands for a mistake I will not make again? I guess my face is going to end up like an old shoe sooner or later, run-down and broken-in—and very comfortable. It'll be nice to have something to show for a lifetime of living.

Life's story, though, is not a puzzle to be worked out, as in that old Fun Book. And I guess the order is linear and sequential, even if we can't always understand that it is. At any rate, it's even more fascinating than fun—for a rainy day!

Middle Distance I

*Y*ou know how sometimes in representational paintings you feel as if you could walk right into them, because the view goes on forever? And then there are others, with a hazy background but a lot of detail catching the eye in the middle distance. The details are usually people. Most commentaries will point out the figures in the middle distance, as if you had trouble with your sight. I guess that's what guides are for.

I think, though, that I sometimes need a guide for my own middle distance. When I step aside and look at my life, there are parts of it I can't see very well.

When you look back at your childhood, it's like looking through one-way glass, watching while you cannot be watched. Your own self back there is like a patient under observation in a clinic. You have all the knowledge of hindsight, oh, and all the compassion in the world for that poor, dumb little creature you used to be, who didn't know which end was up. I feel that way not only about my childhood and teenage years but also about the early years of my marriage and motherhood. It's a view from the wrong end of a telescope, all neat and tiny and tucked away back there, out of reach, and yet still reaching forward and influencing me.

It's easy to tell stories about the distant past. It's also easy to talk about the present, because it is with us right now. Easy to tell what you're doing each day, and not much need to analyze it.

Ah, but when your eye lands on middle distance, that's harder.

Middle Distance II

*Y*esterday I talked about how easy it is to look at our more distant past, like looking through one-way glass, the lessons are all there to be learned. The present, too, is simple to look at, though we know that there are lessons there that we cannot yet assimilate.

The middle distance, though, is harder to look at, harder to understand, harder to absorb. Some artists ignore the middle distance altogether in their landscapes; those who don't are always commented upon.

Somewhere between way back then and now is a middle distance in everyone's life, and it probably has a more profound effect on our present than does the distant past. Middle distance is when present habits were changed or formed. I quit smoking, for example, eleven years ago. That's middle distance—not past, not present, and there are still moments when I would like a cigarette, but I won't take one.

Middle distance is the time when my children began to be human beings in their own right, that is, autonomous individuals with thoughts and impulses I couldn't possibly know, interpret or understand. Middle distance is when I began operating on trust rather than authority. Some call that a safe distance.

I think I might make a lousy painter because my middle distance is still a little chaotic and unformed. I cannot see it whole yet, and the details are murky. It will take more than a few brush strokes to clarify it.

Getting Better, Not Older

*H*ave you heard this definition of getting older? You know you're getting older when you reach the top of the ladder and find it's leaning against the wrong wall. That's sort of depressing, suggesting as it does that all our efforts have been in vain, that we've spent all this time crying after and working for the wrong things.

On the other hand . . .

Look at it this way. Part of the great relief of getting older is finding out how few things are really important. I think it's absolutely delightful when I find myself capable of wearing shoes for comfort and not for appearance—though if I can have both, that's best of all. It's a breakthrough when I, who never missed a party, can skip one in favor of spending time alone with a book or one close friend. And I find myself much more willing and able to listen to other people tell me about their children and their lives, rather than rushing to tell them about mine—sometimes.

So, maybe it's not all bad when we find the ladder leaning against the wrong wall. Maybe, in fact, it's the beginning of wisdom, the realization that the pinnacle we were striving for isn't that important, that the wall we were leaning on wasn't as good a support as we believed, that our feverish climbing can stop now and we can take a look around, and sigh and smile and climb down, if we feel like it, rather than hanging on for dear life.

"Zaccheus," said Jesus, "come down out of that tree!" Maybe He'd tell *us* to get down off that ladder.

Fullness of Joy

The poet Don Marquis said that middle age is waking up and thinking you'll feel better tomorrow. I think a lot of people, no matter what their age, are victims of this attitude—that I'll be better, happier, richer, thinner, whatever, tomorrow, or next week, or some time in the future. Never now.

I think that the "I'll-be-happy-when" attitude is harmful to your health and could be habit-forming. Happiness isn't a product one can actively seek. It sneaks up on you when you aren't looking, and that doesn't happen in the future, it happens in the present.

Watch a child intent on building a sand castle or pouring water in a hole. Seriousness of purpose was never more evident, and yet that total preoccupation with the present moment is a sign of unconscious happiness. Intentness, focus, concentration on something other than one's self, that's what brings about happiness, unbidden and unbought.

Dr. Harold Bloomfield, author of a book called *Inner Joy*, says that pleasure is not a reward for something you do. "It's the primary experience of being alive," he says, and it's essential to health. Bloomfield says that joy doesn't have to be something that happens to you on special occasions, like when you fall in love, or get a raise, or drive your new car for the first time. Rather, it's something you create from moment to moment. It is also a duty.

You don't have to take my word for it; read the Bible, and start counting the number of times we are *told* to rejoice.

"Rejoice in the Lord always: and again I say, rejoice."

What Was Your Name Again?

"*You* haven't changed a bit!"

You've heard people say that, haven't you? People who haven't seen each other for twenty years say that: "You haven't changed a bit!" And their kids stare at them open-mouthed, wondering *how* they can say it, considering the receding or greying hair, the wrinkles, the bulges, the lines and settling that the years have produced.

It's true, though. You still see an essence of the person you knew, the essential person shining through whatever ravages time has wreaked on the body and face. I call it "the two-Certs-in-one syndrome," when you have to make a sudden reconciliation in your perception between the person you remember and the person you see in front of you, twenty years older. It's "two-two-two-Certs-in-one," as the images meld with a click and you see the person whole and steady in the present time.

I think God does that with us, and sees always the real person within. However skinny or fat we become, however life has treated our faces, however we have treated our souls, God sees through all the external images to the genuine essence of our selves. "Two-two-two-Certs-in-one," and we go click into a Master Image, locked in for eternity, and loved.

We should be careful with that essence. We should try not to allow too wide a gap between the real person and the click-in one. It would be *nice* to be the person God sees in us.

13

Count Your Blessings

The nice thing about being my age, and admitting it, is that I can remember things that a lot of you can't because I'm older than you are. I was a little girl when World War II began and a teenager when it ended, so many memories of it are firmly entrenched in my mind.

I was thinking recently of one of the slogans on a poster at the time. It's this:

Use it up
Wear it out
Make it do
Do without

That was designed to make us save on vital materials already in short supply because of the war effort. The ideas in that slogan were not popular after the war. Everyone was delighted to have new things, and such a variety! There were deluxe models and a choice of colors and something to fit every need and every budget, and if it didn't there was always easy credit. The world became our oyster and the pearl was ours— for a price.

And now, suddenly, maybe the price is too high. There is a limit to what we can use and throw away. The world's resources are not infinite. Although it *is* summertime, the livin' is no longer easy, and we have over-extended our credit.

So now we are talking about the energy crisis, and the realization that the economy and our demands on it cannot go on expanding forever. We're coming back, perhaps, in our thinking, to those funny little orders from World War II: Use it up / Wear it out / Make it do / Do without.

Coming in on a Wing and a Prayer

*Y*ou know you're getting old when you know all the words to the funny old songs you hear on the canned music in the super market. I haven't paid close attention to most lyrics for years, but I find myself, unbidden, recalling whole chunks of songs twenty and thirty years old. Sometimes, even more unbidden, I'll find a lump in my throat or tears in my eyes, for no reason, no apparent reason. Has that ever happened to you?

I'm thinking now of some of the lyrics from songs written during World War II. I was still a child when it began, but I was into my teens by the time my father came home from overseas in 1946. It was an emotional time.

"Say a prayer for the boys over there / When they play 'The Maple Leaf Forever.'" "Coming in on a wing and a prayer... / With our full crew aboard / And our trust in the Lord / We're coming in on a wing and a prayer."

I may be wrong, but other than George Harrison's "My Sweet Lord," I think present-day songs are not calling on the Lord or emphasizing the power of prayer so much. I guess it was terrible for songwriters to play with our gut reactions so shamelessly, but maybe that's better than the emptiness of response now.

"Sing aloud unto God our strength; make a joyful noise unto the God of Jacob. Take a psalm, and bring hither the timbrel, the pleasant harp with the psaltery."

We don't need a *war*, we just need some new lyricists.

Who's Ronald Colman?

*L*isten, I've never lied about how old I am, because I'm so bad at arithmetic—I wouldn't be able to adjust historical dates to fit my age! I have a good memory, and if I happen to remember who Ronald Colman was, I can't pretend to be younger than I am.

So that's why I'm going to recall a movie I saw based on the life of the inventor Thomas Edison. As I remember, Mickey Rooney played Edison the boy and Spencer Tracy played the adult. Does anyone else out there remember that?

Of course, I was *very* young, so I don't remember much, but one image has stayed with me ever since. Someone was very sick and had to have emergency surgery on the dining-room table in the middle of the night. Young Tom Edison was hustling around the house gathering up all the candles and kerosene lamps, trying to provide the doctor with enough light. The doctor complained that it still wasn't bright enough for the dangerous, delicate task ahead of him. Then Mickey Rooney / Edison thought of putting a mirror behind all the lamps and candles, thus doubling their effect with the reflected light—bright, bright, shadowless light reflecting from a central source.

It's a wonderful image, and it calls other powerful images to mind. Christ casts no shadows in our lives, but reflects to us the bright light that God shines on us—and we in turn must shine back. Remember the children's hymn, "Jesus Bids Us Shine"? Like a little candle burning in the night.

Christ supplies the mirror, too.

On a Scale of One to Ten...?

There isn't a woman alive who doesn't worry about her physical inadequacy—I mean, her appearance. We've been brainwashed by the media into thinking we are unacceptable as we are, so we exercise and wash and deodorize and make-up, and rearrange our bodies so that men will accept us.

Even the most beautiful women lack total confidence. One will tell you her nose is "funny," another that her teeth are too big; another worries about her hips. All are terrified of aging and the ravages of time.

There isn't one of us who doesn't have some private bane and most of us have more than one. In Bernard Slade's comedy *Same Time Next Year*, George asks Doris, "How can you have such luminous skin in the morning?" and she answers, "I guess God thought chubby thighs were enough."

Each of us would be so gratified if someone would say, "I love you *exactly* the way you are. Thank goodness your nose is so short, your nails so bitten, your hips so broad—that's *exactly* what I love about you!"

That's what God gives us: total acceptance. Whatever we are, do, or have, the total person, flawed as it may be, that's what He loves and accepts. But he accepts more than the warts and the external flaws. He accepts everything about us, from our minor irritabilities to the major sins we've been struggling with for years—harder than hips to reduce!

Accepts us. Loves us. Thank God!

Better or Bigger?

"*E*very day, in every way, I'm getting better and better." That's the attitude of a lot of people these days, not only in terms of their personal lives but also in terms of their material comforts. It has been part of what our neighbors to the south call the American Dream, the idea of the perfectibility of people, coupled with constant improvements in lifestyle. Each person, according to this assumption, has the right to expect that his or her life will be better than that of the preceding generation. The old chicken-in-the-pot idea has been replaced by the two-cars-in-every-garage notion. We have become a nation of conspicuous consumption.

E.F. Schumacher explored some of the economic problems our old attitudes have caused in his book *Small is Beautiful*. The subtitle of the book explained it: *Economics as if People Mattered*. Schumacher was an economist, and he tried in very practical terms to recall us to the kind of economic common sense we need in order to survive as human beings on this earth.

Somewhere along the way, you see, we started thinking that getting better and better meant getting bigger and bigger. We're finally beginning to know better. Maybe the energy crisis will turn out to be a blessing in disguise, if it makes us realize where our energy and strength comes from in the first place—from God.

Better or Thinner?

"Every day, in every way, I'm getting better and better." I said that yesterday, but this isn't a rerun. Yesterday I used that funny, smug little verse to comment on how it affected our attitude towards the economic situation. Today I want to consider how it colors our physical life.

Ten years ago I quit smoking. This is not irrelevant. I have practically cut coffee out of my life, drinking perhaps a cup a week now. I have completely lost my sweet tooth, after years of consciously denying it, and now I never eat chocolate cake or things like that. In fact, I joke, if I live long enough, I'll be perfect!

There's a terrific emphasis on physical fitness now. The most unlikely people are into jogging suits and Adidas and running compulsively on our city streets at ungodly hours of the morning. They wouldn't get up that early to go to church! Men play squash instead of eating lunch. Fitness classes for men and women abound, and many large businesses have launched fitness activities for their employees.

Really diet-conscious at last, people are watching their cholesterol levels, their fat intake, their carbohydrate consumption, and this attention is showing up in insurance charts: people over thirty actually weigh less than they did two or three decades ago. The idea now is, if you become perfect, you'll live longer.

Isn't it time to pay the same assiduous attention to our souls?

Day by Day—Better and Better

"*E*very day, in every way, I'm getting better and better." Yes, I know I said that yesterday and the day before, but Day One I was talking about material things, Day Two I talked about our physical fitness, and now I want to talk about our spiritual life.

The energy crisis has forced us to think about our lifestyle. The emphasis on fitness has forced us to take better care of our bodies. What are we doing about our souls?

When you think of the eagerness with which people begin a new fad diet, or start jogging, or join a fitness class, doesn't it ever make you stop and wonder how they would approach Bible-reading at noon after squash, one day a week of prayer and fasting along with a crash diet, or an early-morning meditation after the jog?

We want our bodies to last long and look good, so we pay the price in terms of effort and attention. We don't seem to care as much about the state of our souls. Somehow, the long-term benefits haven't been made to seem as attractive to us. Poor, ragged, tattered, fat, dirty things—our souls have been terribly neglected. They, too, need a lot of time and attention.

Jesus took forty days and forty nights to get in touch with His soul before He began his active ministry, and He kept in touch through constant prayer. He knew that it takes time, constantly given time and attention.

If we gave our souls that kind of time and attention, we might really get better and better!

It's Never Too Late

*H*ave you ever managed to achieve a change in your life, a real change? I don't mean moving to another city; though that can be a traumatic change, you still take *you* with *you*. I mean an inner change, a change in your habits, your lifestyle.

Specifically now, I'm talking about smoking. A minor item, you may say, and you may say it if you have never smoked. But for thousands of people who are now trying to kick the habit, it is very difficult to do.

I quit smoking almost ten years ago, as a New Year's Resolution. I quit without conviction and with no certainty that I could make it stick. I managed to do it for the first three months with pride and chewing gum; after that it was easy. Then I had to kick the chewing gum habit.

But how wonderful, at a mature age, to be able to change! It was almost worth smoking in order to be able to quit, if you know what I mean. I felt as if I still had some control over my life and my decisions, that it was not too late for me. I need not slide down into middle and old age, a hardened case. If I could quit smoking, there were still other things I could change. What great reassurance that was!

I think that's why God never gives up on us. He knows we *can* change. Selfish, miserable, hardened creatures that we are, set in our ways, impervious to threats and persuasion both, we still have the potential to change our lives for the better. A new life is still possible. It's never too late.

Random Thoughts

I was going through a revolving door recently, and as I noticed how gracefully I did it—after all, I'm old enough to have had years of practice—I wondered if perhaps my first, earliest training for revolving doors wasn't in skipping rope. Remember—those of you who skipped—you were in a line-up, waiting your turn, and when the last person ran out the other side of the rope you had a count of one and then you had to run in and start your number: "Spanish Dancer, touch your toes," or whatever. If you waited too long, you were out; if you timed it wrong, you stopped the rope and you were out. Being out meant you had to take one end of the rope as turner and wait till two other people went out and you could get back in the line again.

Great training for revolving doors. That door, with its four wedges, has to be treated with respect, just like a skipping rope.

Later that same day, I was having my hair cut, and as the helper shampooed my hair, I started wondering whether men whose hands are in hot water all day, like hairdressers' assistants, have a higher threshold for heat than ordinary men. I always figured the reason women are able to grab hot dinner plates and serving dishes without dropping them or yelping with pain is that women's hands are—or used to be—in hot water more. *My* hands used to be impervious. I asked the shampooer about this, but he didn't understand what I was talking about.

The point of all these random thoughts is that each day is an adventure. "The world," as Robert Louis Stevenson wrote, "is so full of a number of things / I'm sure we should all be as happy as kings."

Love and Metrics

*T*hose of you who are over forty, like me, may have begun to feel like permanent aliens on this planet now that the metric changeover in Canada is complete. Perhaps, as I do, you judge the weather now by feel and not by Celsius, and the distances you drive by the time it takes you and not the kilometres, and you cling to your old cookbooks and the fading lines on your old measuring cups.

I guess it all happens by osmosis. Our children and theirs will adapt so quickly, they'll wonder what we mean when we use any of the old sayings based on an earlier system of measurement: "Give 'em an inch and they'll take a mile." "An ounce of prevention is worth a pound of cure." "All wool and a yard wide."

The really impressive thing about changing a whole nation's thinking and functioning is that it can be done. It was a huge task, really, and had to be accomplished by degrees. Road signs and speedometers, measuring equipment, packages and containers, thermometers and scales—everything had to change before people's minds could begin to accommodate a new system.

Wouldn't it be wonderful if we could accomplish such a massive change in our spiritual lives? What if we all really *were* our brother's keeper, and lived it every day?

What would it take to make that happen—and stick? It would affect everything we do as surely as the metric system does. We'd have to start being polite to our family as well as to strangers. We'd have to share our good fortune with those less fortunate. We'd have to reach out to those who need help. We might even start loving our neighbors.

Wait Till the Clouds Roll By

I just realized my umbrella is thirty years old. Isn't that amazing? First, it's an indication of my character that I managed to hang on to it so long. I know a lot of people who have spent their lives leaving a trail of umbrellas behind them. It seems to me every time I move I have four or five umbrellas in the hall closet whose owners have abandoned them without a forwarding address. Not me. I may forget names, but I have never forgotten an umbrella in my life.

Second, it speaks for the quality of my umbrella and for the gentleness with which I have treated it that it is still functional after thirty years. The little brass chain threaded through a hole in the handle by which it could be hung up is gone, but it is still a handsome umbrella— black silk, with lovely petals that furl up nicely and wrap tightly with a self-buttoning ribbon. I bought it on impulse one rainy morning, and my mother was shocked at me for spending so much for an umbrella purchased on the spur of a storm, as it were. Very few possessions, apart from books, have stayed with me for so long.

At the same time, I find it astonishing that it is thirty years old. We take time so much for granted. The years flip by, a decade at a time, it seems, looking back at weather and events that have changed me more than they have changed my umbrella. "To everything there is a season," says Ecclesiastes, "and a time to every purpose under the heaven. . . That which was is now, and that which will be has already been, and God requires that which is past."

And Did Those Feet in Ancient Times...?

*W*hen my son John was a baby, one of my daughters was watching me dress him and asked a question. "When do babies feet stop smelling like roses and start smelling feety?"

It's a good question, and I suppose it's easily answered. When those little rosebud feet begin to support and move their owner about independently, they bear weight and pressure and begin to take on a different shape. They labor and they sweat. And they must be protected from heat and cold and wet and rough paths, and so they are shod in leather (or vinyl, these days). Thus enclosed, they are further shaped and lose their freedom to expand and breathe.

Poor feet! The pressures and confinement and lack of air take the bloom and the fragrance off the rose.

I explained all this to Liz, who, at the busy age of four, had feet that often smelled feety. But every loss is accompanied by a gain. How fortunate are we who have feet, feet that function, feet that take us where we want to go, that make us independent agents, free to explore and wander as well as to stand and serve.

And how fortunate is anyone who can stand on his own two feet. Better, as the old saying goes, to have one good foot than two crutches. How are *your* poor feet? It's not so bad if they no longer smell like roses, but do watch it that they're not made of clay.

Remember Isaiah: "How beautiful upon the mountains are the feet of him that bringeth good tidings, that publisheth peace."

Yes I Can

Remember the game Giant Steps? The person who was IT stood at the end of the field, and all the slaves lined up at the starting line far away.

"Betty Jane," IT would call. "You may take two Baby Steps."

"May I?" you asked.

You had to ask for confirmation, or permission was automatically denied. Even then, the answer was not certain. "Yes, you may" was what you hoped to hear, but "No, you may not" could still happen.

There was a variety of Steps possible: Baby Steps, Scissor Steps, Sideways Steps, Backward Steps, Giant Steps. Best of all, of course, were Giant Steps.

The purpose of the game was to make it up front and become IT, and then it was your turn to dole out the favors.

IT had to be very watchful. People could sneak up on IT when IT wasn't looking, when IT was watching someone else take his allotted steps. If the sneakers were caught by IT, they had to go back to the start. But if they had ceased to move before IT noticed, then it was too late.

You and I, we're still playing the game, aren't we? We keep asking for permission to make our moves, pretending that external circumstances prevent us from doing what we should. I suppose the way we move says something about us, too. "Take two Giant Steps." "May I?" "No, you may not."

What are you going to do about it?

Adult's Play

*D*o you remember the game Scissors-Paper-Rock? You play it with your hands: the players pound one fist against the other to a count of three and then simultaneously they illustrate the instrument of their choice with one hand on the other fist. An open, flat hand means paper; two fingers in a V become scissors; the clenched fist retained is a rock. The rules are: paper covers rock, scissors cut paper, rock crushes scissors. Whoever wins the round gets to administer a swift whip of two wet fingers across the other person's wrist. If you don't have a little ESP or a lot of luck, you could end up with a stinging wrist. It's quite a vicious game, actually. Kids love it.

So do grown-ups, but they don't play it with their hands, and the penalties they administer are tougher than a wet-fingered flick on the wrist. Why do we play life so hard? We seem to expect vindictiveness on all sides, and feel justified when we dish it out ourselves.

What's wrong with being gentle for a change? There are all kinds of ways to stop playing Scissors-Paper-Rock. Let someone with only one or two packages ahead of you and your crowded cart in the supermarket. Smile back instead of frowning at the stranger who gives you a tentative smile on the street. Be polite and give your time to someone who asks you for directions. Thank the long-distance operator and comment on his or her accuracy and care. Be patient with a slow clerk, an old person or a tired child. You might even avoid getting *your* wrist slapped.

Help! I'm a Prisoner in a Baby Factory!

*I*t's funny how fast you forget things, even searing experiences you yourself have gone through. Recently I was visiting with some friends who are younger than me, so young, in fact, that they are expecting their second child. It had been a hectic week for the couple, and their first child was showing the effects that they, in their maturity, were attempting to hide.

But pregnancy has a volatile nature, and something happened to cause the young woman to break down. Yes, break out, in tears and emotion and a need to escape. The only trouble was, with one small child already in the home, there isn't any place to escape to. You can't abandon the child, and there's no place to hide.

She said to me, "I feel so trapped!"

I'd forgotten that feeling, actually forgotten it. But it all came rushing back to me then.

Remember?

If you're a young or expectant mother now, you know firsthand what I'm talking about. You are trapped inside that ungainly body, trapped in your motherhood, in your marriage. In everything you always wanted, you feel trapped. You don't really want out, you don't want it all to go away forever—just for a little while, just for the moment, just for a few delicious hours of carefree escape, when you can push responsibility aside and pretend you're free again. Free—whatever that means.

Suddenly I remembered one night at the dinner table, surrounded by my husband and three darling children and pregnant with a fourth child, suddenly being overwhelmed by it all, wanting desperately to get away. Know what I did?

I left my family.

I left them. I put on my coat and walked out of the house—and walked around the block. Then I came home and helped clean up the kitchen, put my kids to bed and sat down for the evening with my husband.

That's all.

Not much of a moral there, I suppose. You just keep on keeping on, living by your commitment, taking the thick with the thin, hanging in there, loving inch by inch, and living your love.

Bless Me!

*D*o you know of any saints who were married women?

Hagiologists—people who study saints—could probably tell me of married women who were saints, but I suspect that they were wives first and saints second. You read of women in ages past who, when their lovers or husbands died, entered convents and led exemplary lives. God didn't even seem to mind that He was their second choice.

I wonder, I really do wonder, if it is possible to be a wife and mother and come anywhere close to saintliness. It is so easy to love in a vacuum. The hard part begins when you have to love someone who tracks mud on your clean kitchen floor, makes plaster of paris in your mixing bowl and never hangs up a towel or makes his bed. Or to feel saintly at all times about someone who leaves his shaved bristles in the bathroom basin, squeezes the toothpaste from the middle of the tube and refuses to set a good example for the children by eating up all his squash and brussels sprouts.

Married women don't get to make spectacular sacrifices or appeal to thousands on an emotional level. They just get up in the night for one hungry baby or one sick child, and they feed one family three meals a day every day for years and years and years. And they yell and holler and complain—and carry on. Yes, they do carry on, bless them.

I Was Held Up at the Office

I was trapped in a meeting the other day for twice as long as I expected to be—four hours instead of two—and other people were waiting for my call and my appearance to do something I had promised to do for them. My son Matthew, along with a friend of mine and her two small boys, were waiting for me to take them swimming and feed them hamburgers. They waited and waited and I didn't call.

For my part, I was torn by a lot of emotions and pressures. I was learning a new skill, one I haven't had much practice in—writing for film—so I couldn't afford to cut the session short. Nor could I get to a phone. I was fighting for my professional life. On the other hand, I knew that people were waiting for me and wondering what was keeping me, and I felt guilty and responsible for their happiness that day because of my promise to them.

And then I thought of men. It's a cliché, isn't it? The wife with a burnt dinner on the stove, waiting forever for her husband to come home: "Where were you? Why didn't you call? You knew I was expecting you."

And I thought that at last, women, in their new role as the breadwinner—some of them the sole support of a family—women in this role are experiencing the other side of that situation: a meeting one cannot leave, a phone call that cannot be made, an emotional pressure and a personal demand that cannot, for the moment, be met.

I've seen both sides now, both sides of the burnt dinner, and we should all be so fortunate, because it helps to develop some compassion and sympathy, and those are things we all need a lot of.

Volcano Scapegoat?

*I*f you live near a volcano you always have something to blame for your troubles. That's what psychologists found out when they interviewed residents of seven towns within 40 or 90 miles of Mount St. Helen's volcano after its eruptions.

Subjects chosen randomly by telephone who agreed to follow-up interviews blamed everything from stomach aches to marital problems on the volcano. They ran out of time, they didn't eat as well, their houses were dirtier, they were more tired, less efficient, had too much to do, didn't eat or sleep as well, and had more fights with their mates. Only one man said he thought the volcano had helped clear up his skin disorder.

I guess we all have a volcano in our lives, maybe several of them. Something we can blame for our problems, errors, faults, and delays. Few of us are ready to take the blame squarely on ourselves for almost anything that happens to us. There are always other circumstances conveniently at hand to blame.

Does it make us any happier, do you think? Is it easier to blame something else than to blame ourselves? If we blamed ourselves, we might have to do something to change, and that would be not only time-consuming and a nuisance, but it might also be painful. Easier to go on finding convenient volcanoes to get mad at.

Well, no one can stop a volcano from erupting, but while it may seem almost as difficult when we start, we can change ourselves. Look inside yourself for signs of eruption, then find the still centre and cling to it.

And Who Gets Custody of You?

With the divorce rate increasing all the time, happily married couples are beginning to feel as if they're walking on the edge of a precipice. "What are we doing right?" they wonder, and "When is it going to stop?" One mis-step and they, too, may topple into the ranks of disgruntled singles.

Were most marriages always unhappy and it is only because divorce is relatively easy now that people no longer have to put up with wrangling and incompatibility, betrayal and mental cruelty, and by a decree, end a relationship that is supposed to be a sacrament? Do people now demand more and give less, and give up when the going gets tough? If people and relationships turn sour, is the sourness in the eye of the beholder or do we *cause* it to happen in the person we behold?

Helmet Thielicke in his book *How the World Began* comments on this: He asks, "Have I perhaps caused (the other person) to become what perhaps he really has become? The other person, whom God has joined to me, is never what he is apart from me. He is not only bone of my bone; he is also boredom of my boredom and lovelessness of my lovelessness."

We have the same responsibility in our relationship with God. If we do not feel loved, it is because we have not returned His love, and have not allowed His love for us to encompass us. If we are tired of life, it is not because the life He has given us is so tiring, but because we have rejected the life-force and energy He makes available to us.

Burnout I

urnout—that's the expression now for the effects of too much stress on the job. As reported in the magazine *Psychology Today*, workshops designed to prevent burnout have been conducted by a team comprised of a social worker and a psychologist in the U.S. In one experiment, the participants were asked to list their images of what burnout meant to them. They came up with an interesting set of metaphors. Here's burnout:

- an empty well
- a checking account with frequent withdrawals and few deposits, maybe even an overdraft
- an overstretched rubber band
- a wrung-out dishrag
- a rag doll or stuffed toy with half the stuffing gone
- wilted flowers
- meeting a brick wall
- always meeting Dead End signs
- being trapped on a railroad track with a freight train coming
- feeling trapped, as a mouse being teased by a cat
- caught in a whirlpool or on a treadmill
- needing to escape—crawling into a hole and pulling it in after you
- being a turtle in a shell and pulling in your head
- going to bed with the covers over your head
- giving up: drowning / bleeding to death / swinging like a yo-yo at the end of the string.

Let's try for the antidote tomorrow.

Burnout II

esterday I was telling you about some of the images that people with stressful jobs use to describe their situation when they have reached a point known as burnout, that is, the inability to go on under such circumstances. The article I read in *Psychology Today* listed all the metaphors suggested by participants in a workshop dealing with burnout, but the article gave no solutions. I'll try to.

I've reached the point often enough myself—I guess we all have. Currently, I'm comparing it to landing on a space platform and not knowing where I'm going next, but knowing that the first step will be a big one. A bit fearful, at that. So what do I do?

Well, I make a cup of tea and I write in my diary. I do recommend that. Paper is my friend, and it could be yours. If you write down what's bothering you, that's a good step. At least you can identify the enemy. Usually, it's you, yourself.

I know, I know *truly* that God is the source of my strength and power and light, and that all I have to do is keep my channel open, keep my chimney clear and let the power flow through, let the light shine forth. But I forget. Just like Peter, when he was walking on the water, I look down and get confused, lose my confidence and flounder. My channel fills up with silt, my chimney gets covered with soot and I have to start dredging and polishing.

How? Well, I read the Bible. And I pray. And I talk to people. And I write. And then I do something for someone else, to get the power flowing again. And I hang in there.

How To Have a
Heart Attack

ere's another list for you. These are things to do to bring on a heart attack:

- think of or do two things at once
- schedule more and more activities into less and less time
- fail to notice or be interested in your surroundings or things of beauty
- hurry the speech of others
- become irritated when forced to wait in line or when driving behind a car you think is moving too slowly
- believe that if you want something done well you have to do it yourself
- gesticulate when you talk
- jiggle your knees or tap your fingers frequently
- break into explosive speech patterns or obscenities
- make a fetish of being always on time
- have difficulty sitting and doing nothing
- play nearly every game to win, including games with children
- measure your own and others' success in terms of numbers, i.e., numbers of patients seen, reports written, pies baked, whatever
- click your lips, nod your head, clench your fists, pound the table or suck in air when you're speaking
- become impatient watching others do things you think you can do better or faster
- blink your eyes rapidly or lift your eyebrows, almost like a tick

There. These are all kinds of behavior that could cause heart attacks. They are also, if you noticed, besides being self-damaging, extremely self-centered and self-seeking, just plain selfish.

"Be still, and know that I am God."

Blue Genes?

*H*ave you ever heard people say they thought they were born tired? Well, I think some people are born happy.

You must have met someone like that, a person who, in defiance of all hard facts, continues to be cheerful and to look on the bright side? Disaster does seem to dog some people's footsteps and yet some people insist on smiling in the face of adversity and carry on with their lives with more that dogged persistence—with downright enthusiasm.

On the other hand, you've met people who are never happy, never satisfied. This one was born with a silver spoon in his mouth, has been given every advantage, has the world by the tail and yet he complains all the time. He doesn't know what the world is coming to, people are not to be trusted, business going to the dogs, help is incompetent, his children are ungrateful and his wife is a bore. Does he bring it on himself, or was it programmed into his nature?

It makes you wonder whether happiness is in the genes rather than in circumstances. Is there a chromosome for smiles, a particular DNA combination for optimist, a complex one for gloom? I hope not. It *is* possible for people to change their attitudes. Psychologists have proved that happy behavior can lead to a happier frame of mind. You may not be able to change circumstances but surely it is possible to change your reaction to them. I'd hate to think I had no control over my laughter and tears. The only blue genes I'll accept are the ones I wear.

Wait! I've Got a Knot in My Thread!

I like the children's story in the church service because I understand it best, and also because it usually has a concrete example, and I think I have a concrete mind.

I remember one time the minister picked up the embroidered cloth hanging on the lectern—the one you see marked IHS. The minister showed the kids the underside of the embroidery. It was neat, because the person who did the needlework was meticulous and painstaking. But it was unintelligible. You could not make out legible letters, and there were many threads crossing others on their way to a new entry point on the front of the work.

Life, pointed out the minister to the kids and me, is like that. God is the craftsman working out a design, and we are the threads He works with. When we look at it, we can't understand it, because we are on the wrong side of the finished design. So it seems to us to be an incomprehensible maze of threads crossing and crisscrossing with no pattern or intent. This is our people's-eye- or maybe our thread's-eye-view of God's wonderful design, which only He, in His infinite wisdom, can conceive in its entirety.

I'd like to take it one step further and say that sometimes we see what we think is the right side of a design, and it still doesn't make any sense to us. That's because the designers are not as skilled as God is. We never have a grasp of the whole design; at best, we can put a neat thread in here and there and hope it won't clash with the ultimate purpose. Trust the infinite designer.

Wonder

"Except ye be as a child, ye shall not enter the Kingdom of Heaven." I was thinking of those words of Jesus's lately, being as it's summer holidays and all, and kids are sort of underfoot. There are definitely more dirty glasses in the sink, and if you're anywhere near sand, you'll be familiar with a gritty shuffle underfoot as well. Obviously, Jesus did not have dirty glasses and sand in mind when He talked about entering the Kingdom.

What then, are the qualities a child has that we all must have? What's so special about children that we should try to copy them instead of always trying to get them to hang up their clothes and come when they're called?

A sense of wonder, for one thing. You can find a child staring at an anthill, or for that matter an ant, for hours on end, with wonder and patience and awe, and he will then proceed to tell you more details about an ant than you care to know.

I looked up "wonder" in the Oxford English Dictionary. It defines wonder as "astonishment mingled with perplexity or bewildered curiosity." That surely is the state with which we will contemplate the Kingdom of Heaven. The thought of Heaven, even with all the stereotypes surrounding it today, surely breeds astonishment, and the perplexity we suffer as to whether it exists geographically and whether we qualify for entrance, leaves us all in a permanent state of bewildered curiosity. That is the kind of wonder, if we're lucky, that we share with children and that begins to make us eligible for Heaven.

Paris Green?

I've been thinking about envy recently. At its worst, envy is really dissatisfaction with one's self. If one were at rest, totally, one would not have to dress ranks, that is, compare one's self with others. But if we constantly find that such comparisons put us at a disadvantage, feel ourselves falling short of others' apparent perfections, we'll never recognize our own genuine achievements and myriad blessings.

You know how, when you're planning ahead a little, you say to yourself, "Now, if I could just lose ten pounds, I'd be happy," or "If I could get just one more raise in pay, I'd be okay," or "If I had a color TV like the Joneses, I could put the old one in the bedroom and watch the news in bed" or whatever. All these material plans of ours spring from a dissatisfaction with what we already have.

What we need is not more things, or achievements, or good looks, but a really hard look at our values.

Maybe what we need more than another TV is to spend more time with our kids. Maybe more than a crash diet, we need to change our eating habits.

Nothing is simple, is it? We can't even indulge in a little old-fashioned green-eyed envy without having to reverse its aim and see where it came from. Because the person envy hurts most is one's self.

Recently, I sent a card to a successful colleague. It says, "Congratulations! I always knew someone I admired would be rich and famous one day." And inside, it says, "But, somehow I thought it would be me!"

41

Blackmail

*H*ave you got troubles? I guess everybody has.

When a nephew of mine was a little boy he went to visit his grandmother while his parents were on a trip. One evening he misbehaved at the dinner table and he was sent to his room. There he started listing his troubles in a loud voice.

"Here I am," he said, with a convincing quaver in his voice. "All alone. My mother and father are far away, and I'm all alone." Pause. "I haven't had any dinner and I'm hungry." Pause. "Have you ever heard a sadder story in your life?"

His grandmother, in fact, was standing outside the door of his room with a tray of food, as grandmothers are wont to do. She heard every word of his sad, manipulative story and broke up—in laughter. His sad tale, duly repeated, became a family joke in our house.

Whenever I am tempted to feel really sorry for myself, I remember my nephew's words and come up short. Self-pity is a cheap form of self-dramatization and it's about as convincing as that five-year-old's hard luck story. Not only that, it's emotional blackmail.

Have you ever heard a sadder story in your life?

You can have those words. Save them for your next rainy day, and use them well. Turn them on yourself, listen for that quaver, and try to laugh.

Waltz Me Around Again, Linda!

When I left Stratford I had the biggest garage sale in the world, and I've written about that before—how one man's junk is another man's precious possession, and about how careful we should be about the junk we choose to keep, both material and spiritual. Now I want to tell you about Linda.

Linda was a giant papier-mâché doll my daughter Liz made for a school project. She had a shelf in her stomach designed to hold a tape recorder. At school, Linda and Liz conducted a history quiz about famous Canadian women. Graduated, she became my son Matthew's property, and he used to tape screams and strangling sounds for poor Linda to cope with. She used to go out on the porch on Hallowe'en armed with a full set of eerie sound effects and became a popular neighborhood wonder.

No one bought Linda at our garage sale, and she certainly couldn't go with us to a crowded city apartment. So on Monday morning after the sale, she went out on the street for pick-up by the garbage detail. Her last minutes were witnessed by a neighbor. The big white truck pulled up, followed by the men feeding it. One of the men picked up Linda, held her lightly in a graceful waltz grip and danced her round the street! Then, gently, she was fed into the maw of the garbage truck.

We were all comforted that she was paid such respect right up to the end. The incident also gave me further respect for garbagemen. People are interesting, aren't they? And nice, too.

All That Garbage

*Y*ou all know about garage sales—you know about mine, too, because I've told you about it before. But garage sales have been on my mind again, I think because it's time I had another one, except that I don't have a garage any more.

I had the biggest garage sale in the world, but I guess it wasn't big enough. At the time I thought it was. I was squeezing from a ten-room house to a city apartment. I was selling not only my past but also a lot of my future, because life had written me a different script and I needed different—and fewer—props.

My garage sale paid for my move, but it did more than that. It was a symbolic ending to my other life. I finally had not only the necessity but the courage to divest myself of more than half of my possessions.

It's a very freeing thing, and I have never looked back. I have never wondered whatever happened to such-and-such, or who bought the whatsis. Of course I had friends acting as sales clerks and did not personally oversee each sale myself, so that saved a few pangs, too.

The only thing I had to get back was a new broom belonging to my neighbor. She had used it the night before to sweep out my garage and left it leaning on the wall and someone bought it for a dollar. But I have not regretted anything of mine. It wasn't mine any-more. I'm traveling lighter now, no longer attached to THINGS . . . ah, but still weighted down. I really need another garage sale. You should try one, too—good for your soul.

A Moving Story

I remember when we were moving from Winnipeg to Stratford, we had to consolidate our resources—that means, I had to get rid of a lot of stuff. One does when one moves.

My daughter Kate was a little young to understand this, at age eleven. Besides, she had an eclectic approach to life, even at that age. So she prepared to move to another province in her own way. She was going to pack her own things. I came with boxes and a desire to guide when she had barely begun.

She had a small box and in it she had already packed two stubby crayons, an invitation to a birthday party she had attended the week before, a doll's dress, three hair clips, one of them broken, and a couple of sheets of paper with schoolwork on them.

I unpacked for her. I threw out the crayons, the schoolwork and the broken hairclip, put the two good ones into her brush-and-comb bag, the doll's dress in the trunk of dolls' clothes, the invitation in her scrap-book box and gave her a lecture.

"You are not moving to a new province," I said, "by taking your Manitoba gumbo with you. You must be more organized."

Well, she wasn't. The gumbo came with us all, I'm afraid. Sometimes I think I'll drown in it, drown in a sea of gumbo, all the unrelated bits and pieces of my past that stick to me like mud.

You'll be happy to know that Kate is more organized than I am now, though still charmingly eclectic. We all drag our past around with us, and maybe it's a good thing. It gives us roots.

Another Moving Story

*R*oots. I was talking about the things we take with us when we move, and suggesting, perhaps, a need to get organized. But then again, I'm not so sure. Things are what keep us anchored and, maybe, stable.

Attics are almost a thing of the past. Many people have relegated to garages and carport storage boxes, or even to car trunks, the things they used to keep in attics. Basements aren't bad, though you hear horror stories about flash floods and sewers backing up, thus ruining priceless albums of matchbook covers or, in one sad case I know of, a woman's *Gone With the Wind* paper dolls. Sigh.

We're all squirrels, aren't we? Or magpies, maybe, saving bits of string and shiny coins and bright baubles of remembrances, saving the old rocker till we have grandchildren to rock in it, saving the snowshoes in case we ever get the urge and opportunity to strike out on deep snow, saving the metronome because we might need to mark time again, saving too many vases for all the flowers we hope to put in them, old 78-rpm records we'll never play because they're clunky and scratchy and we'll never replace them because we already have them. All these things anchor us, because they give us a past.

They also make it hard to move.

I wonder if, properly used, such mementos might actually slow the divorce rate?

Mirrors

You may know the Ontario Science Centre, with its touch-me, play-me, work-me exhibits. It was there that I finally decided to have all my hair cut off, when I caught inadvertent glimpses of myself in unexpected mirrors.

There's a bicycle you pedal until you generate enough power to see yourself dimly on a TV screen, and it's a shock to see that earnest face, its occupant intent on pumping herself into visibility. In my case, it was a shock to see my long, messy hair. Then there's another exhibit you walk through, with slanted floors that make you seem to grow larger or smaller, and you see yourself in a mirror in relation to this strange room you're in—again, I decided the hair had to go.

If you want to see yourself as others see you, go to the Science Centre and catch yourself unawares. All the other mirrors we use at home, and in public washrooms, too, receive a prepared image of us. The Science Centre mirrors, because they are unexpected and because we are intent on something other than ourselves, are more likely to catch us as we really are.

Nietzsche said, "We all get the faces we deserve." Tell me truly: do you feel you deserve the face you have? Is there something about it you would change? Is it a happy face? Resigned? Sad? Bitter? When you catch it when it doesn't know you're looking, does it tell you and other people things you'd rather not reveal? What have you been doing all these years that made your face what it is today? Take a look at yourself. Does *your* hair need cutting?

Love Me As I Am

My grandmother Tergesen was a little old lady when she died. She was one of the few women in my family who died before her husband. Much as I sorrow over the fact that women tend to outlive their men now, I can see why it's a kindness on the part of God. Grandpa was lost without Grandma. He turned his chair to the window and looked out in silence when he sat in the evenings, gazing in the direction of the cemetery, though it was nowhere in sight. I remembered him when my husband died, and felt an odd kind of gratitude that Bill was spared the pain of losing me.

Grandma had an open casket in the house for friends and relatives to come and say goodbye. Grandpa kept tiptoeing into the living room where the casket was, to take a peek at Grandma while she was still there.

He had married her when he was nineteen and she seventeen. That had been some sixty-odd years before, yet he still saw her as she was. I came into the room shortly before the people started arriving for the service and he said to me, "Doesn't she look beautiful?—just like a young girl." That's how he still saw her, after all those years.

I think God sees us that way. He loves us so much that He sees us at our best, open and fresh, unscarred and unsoiled, and *young*, forever young in innocence and love.

I Kill Bugs, Too

Albert Schweitzer always used to bother me. The world-famous man who gave up a career as a musician, theologian, philosopher and academic to become a mission doctor serving remote people in Africa, called himself a mass-murderer of microbes, who justified that killing only because he was saving human lives. It was Schweitzer who coined the phrase "a reverence for life," and he not only said it, he lived it.

He won the Nobel peace prize in 1952, the year I got married, and I really wondered if I was doing the right thing. My diary from those early days of marriage has entries about Albert Schweitzer. I felt guilty because of what *he* had done, turning his back on the world and material success and fame and burying himself in Africa to occupy himself in a lifelong battle with leprosy, sleeping sickness and all the tropical diseases that wiped out entire tribes.

Well, Albert Schweitzer still bothers me, and I guess he should. I plugged along, stayed married to one man until his death, raised four children, taught Sunday school. I write a little. That's all. We more common people swell ranks, though, and we have to try to do our job, however simple and unimportant it may seem. People like Albert Schweitzer remain a shining example to us all.

Who Is the Greatest Lover of Them All?

*I*t was one of those male/female relationship articles that women's magazines are full of, assigning different strengths of love to different relationships. In every relationship, this article claimed, there is always one who loves more. It went on to illustrate this by asking the reader to choose the one who gave or loved more in famous contemporary relationships, as, for example, Jacqueline Kennedy and John Kennedy, Jacqueline Onassis and Aristotle Onassis. If you've picked the one who seemed more loving in each of those pairs, you're onto the point, such as it is.

The article continued by asking the reader to decide which of a loving pair she would rather be, the more loving or more receiving of love?

At some point, I think several generations before this one, women, particularly, might have chosen to be the more loving. We were taught that it was better to give than receive. We knew what it was like to be overwhelmed and overflow with love and good will towards our loved ones and our community family.

Within the church and the larger community, both men and women operate on an assumption of service to one's fellows. I'm not sure that such an assumption exists any more.

If we now prefer to be loved more than we love, if we want someone to sacrifice more for us than we are prepared to sacrifice for them, we don't have far to look. God is such a lover. He loves us beyond our human capacity even to understand such love, and the sacrifice Jesus made for us has to be all that anyone could hope for.

The Power of Love

I talked to a man recently who is afraid of heights but who went not once but twice on a hideous roller coaster ride to show his son there was nothing to be afraid of. He gritted his teeth, put his stomach down where he hoped it would stay, and hung on. I think it may be misplaced masculinity based on the idea that boys/men are not supposed to cry or be frightened, but the man's action is another example of what you will do for love.

For himself, he wouldn't have gone near that roller coaster ride. For his son, he braved it twice. He transcended his fear, he surpassed himself. Not only is that an illumination of the power of love, it also reveals the meaning of sacrifice. And the whole meaning of sacrifice is that it must have a meaning.

There's an old joke about someone who got up early to stand in line to get tickets to a show he wanted to take his wife to for her birthday. "I wouldn't get up this early for a job," joked the man. That's the whole point of sacrifice.

It really is staggering, the power of love. Awesome. Tiny little examples like these only hint at the strength and power waiting to be released, strength and power that are based on love. Little by little we can begin to appreciate this explanation from the book of John:

"For God so loved the world that He gave His only begotten son that whosoever believed in him should not perish but should have everlasting life."

That's love!

Old Habits Can Be Replaced As Well As Pans

*T*his story is now a national myth.

The home economist of a national women's magazine was interviewing a young married woman in a survey of cooking habits and asked her why she cut the bone off the end of a ham before she baked it. The young woman replied that that was what her mother always did. The home economist then interviewed the mother and asked the question again, and the reply was the same—because *her* mother always did that. The grandmother was alive and well and living in the same city, so the economist went to her and put the question again: "Why do you cut the bone off the end of the ham?"

"Because my pan is too short," the old woman said. We do have to learn to throw out old assumptions in everything we do.

In these days of women's liberation, women are learning to come to terms with their mothers as they have not done before in this century. They are trying not to repeat to their daughters the tones and patterns of recrimination of their mothers and grandmothers before them.

It took *years* for my mother and me to come to terms with each other, to reach the point of friendship and love and acceptance that we enjoy now. It took much less time for my daughters to come to terms with me. That's because they're smarter than I am, and stronger, but also because they had this new notion of feminism to help them. They had the courage to become themselves and assert their autonomy, independent of me.

"All women become like their mothers—that is their tragedy," wrote Oscar Wilde. "No man does—that's his." Clever, but perhaps it's no longer true. My daughters have become like themselves, God bless them.

Communication is Another Way of Saying Hello

*P*eople talk so much about communicating these days. Do they know what they're saying? Younger people, fearful of their first commitments, talk about the need to communicate. Business people feel they must communicate, both with their clients or customers and with their staff, in order to understand their needs and promote trust between them. Married couples go to marriage counselors, troubled because they are not communicating as they should be. We call the media—radio, TV, newspapers, magazines, books, etc.—the communication art forms, and judge them for their effectiveness in communicating, that is, in conveying information and ideas, to say nothing of prejudices and judgements.

But do we know what communication really is? I came across a definition of it that I want to share with you. "Direct communication," said American theatre teacher Viola Spolin, "is a moment of mutual perceiving."

First, you see, real communication occurs only for a moment. A moment of insight, a moment of perception—a flash, if you will. Add up enough such moments or flashes and you have, if you're lucky, enough illumination to light you on your way.

Second, communication is *mutual* perceiving. It has to take place between two people simultaneously. Married couples are right to worry about their lack of communication. If it isn't mutual, they do not, indeed, have a marriage. Nor does any one of us have a relationship with anyone else without mutual perceptions. Our eyes may be focused on different things but our minds are in tune with each other. It's great with people, and of course—need I say?—with God.

Scrapbook History

*M*y entire life is in boxes and scrapbooks, that is, what isn't in my diaries. Well-documented, you might say. But unorganized. I almost never throw away a piece of paper. It gets to be a terrible burden.

The last time I caught up with my boxes was 1967. One of these days I think I'm going to catch up again, take them out, sort out all the stuff and paste it into scrapbooks. I'll let you know in time so that you can buy shares in a glue company.

Other people, including my children, scoff at me, but if they find pictures of themselves they stop to examine them, and they marvel over a World War II ration book or War Savings Stamp, and shake their heads in wonder over the prices in a menu from a bygone luxury hotel or restaurant.

I have notes passed to me in school from people who have become lifelong friends as well as from people I have never seen again. I have flowers pressed from long-forgotten dances—a far cry from the hustle at the singles' bar today.

If you ever want a brief social history, just take a look at my scrapbooks. And boxes.

The things I treasure most are notes—funny or thoughtful gestures that reaffirm my essential belief in people's kindness. For years I kept an egg, hard-boiled, with a crayon face and a plasticine nose on it, telling me that I was a "good egg"—until it cracked and the smell forced its premature retirement to a garbage can.

We all carry our pasts in our present, of course, but when you have whole scrapbooks and boxes full of history, the past seems closer and more friendly.

Unsafe At Any Speed

*Y*ears ago now, I had a Volkswagen car. It was a little like those circus cars that you can stuff twenty-seven people and a dog into. At the lake we used to put little kids in the back shelf with the groceries, and stack them three deep in the back seat, with a child on the lap of the adult in the passenger front bucket and only the driver with nothing to hold onto except the steering wheel. It was a great car, and it took me through a lot.

My oldest daughter Liz had turned sixteen and learned to drive. At last! There was one child who no longer needed to be driven to her music lesson on the outskirts of town, or picked up at her allergy shot in order to get to a swimming meet on time. I was set to toss Liz the keys to the Volkswagen and let her drive herself to her music lesson when I had a sudden thought—or rather, several rushes of thoughts. Because I realized I had to explain to her how to jolly the car along, how you had to double-clutch to shift into second, and how you had to be careful on curves because the steering was a bit sluggish, and don't try to jump a stoplight or beat another car on a turn because the pick-up wasn't that great, or even reliable and you might end up stalled instead. And then I thought, if the car is so unsafe for Liz to drive, what am I doing driving it? The car was too old and had to go.

But we do that with a lot of things. We tell our kids not to do something because it's unsafe, or dangerous, or could get them into trouble. But what about us? If it's so bad for our kids, then why isn't it bad for us, too? Some things are unsafe at any speed—or age.

Here I Am

My mother never wanted anyone to know how old she was. She was of the generation that believed what Oscar Wilde said: "A woman who would tell you her age will tell you anything."

In her eighties, my mother said to me, "You know, there's still a young person inside me. I don't feel old at all. I'm the same person I always was."

The reason that impressed me was that my daughter Liz said much the same thing to me. She was about twenty-four when she wrote me a letter and said she still "felt nine years old, playing Barbie dolls on Centennial Street."

That's when I realized that I feel the same way. Inside me, there is still a wide-eyed young person who never quite knows what's going on. I feel the way I felt when I was little and trying to catch the attention of a salesclerk to wait on me.

That's funny, isn't it? We have all presented different faces to the world, my mother, my daughter and I. But inside, essentially, we are still young and full of wonder and trying to figure out what to do next.

Somehow, I think that inside picture is the accurate one—the essence of us. It's the one that God sees. He knows who we are and why we're here. He sees the child in us, even when it seems to have disappeared in the eyes of the world.

Well, they say you're only as old as you feel. If you feel as young and as incompetent as I do, then I guess we all qualify as children, don't we? Thank goodness.

Welcome Home

*S*ome of you may remember when my second daughter, Kate, went off on an extended trip last year. She graduated from university, worked for the summer and then took a backpack and bedroll, a Eurail pass, a Youth Hostel card and her life's savings to go and explore Europe and the Near East while she discovered herself. I prayed for her safe return and let her go.

Well, she came back. Eight months later she came back, with an even bigger smile, a wealth of stories and memories, dozens of new friends from all over the world and a new self-confidence and strength that sit well on her young shoulders.

I haven't begun to hear all her experiences, probably never will. She's still half-sorry to be home, and missing her new friends, while happy to see old ones and her family again. It's a difficult adjustment for her, in fact, this re-entry to a life that went on without her, but one she is coping with with her customary grace.

I just want to say how grateful I am that she's back. We must send our children away, I know that. A parent is not successful if the birds don't leave the nest and learn to fly by themselves—but so far? Still, you have to let them go. And still, I say it's nice to have them back.

All life is like that, isn't it? A going and a returning, a constant letting go and receiving again. We all grow and change, and we only really grow because of change.

And some days our children grow up, just like that.

Goodbye Again

As my children grow ever older, more independent and more adventurous, it seems to me I'm always saying goodbye to one or another of them. If your children are as old as mine, you probably are, too. One just comes home and another goes off, and you have another clutch of fear to deal with, an apprehension for their safety that you must put to rest, somehow.

A friend once told me that if she thought of the worst thing that could happen, it never happened. It was only when she felt lulled by what turned out to be a false sense of security, thinking nothing could go wrong, that things went wrong. I don't think that's any guarantee.

My father used to say that just when people seem to have made it, to be free from worry and care, that's when they should look out because something bad was bound to happen. And he was right. It did. But he said that you should be grateful if you have troubles because they're insurance that nothing further can happen. That's not true, I have discovered. When things are bad, as bad as you think they can be, it's perfectly possible for them to get worse.

No—there are no talismans against disaster. But you *can* pray. Not a "gimme" prayer, but a prayer of acceptance. "If it be *Thy* will, let this child come safely home"—but that's all. Send your children with God and pray for the strength to bear the parting, whether temporary or permanent. God go with them, and with you, till you meet again.

I Was a Stranger in Your Midst

*A*while ago I left home to live for three weeks on the Old Age Pension, to see what it's really like to live alone in a room with no other resources than a government payment. During that time I attended a neighborhood church, wearing my tacky clothes borrowed from the donations room of a women's hostel and using an assumed name. I wondered how I would be treated.

I was invited for coffee, and winced because it cost a quarter. That first week I wasn't sure I could afford such luxuries. But I sipped my coffee and made conversation as people approached. I was invited to join a group and given the date, time and place for the next meeting.

The following week, a few people remembered my borrowed name and greeted me warmly. Two choir members invited me to come out for choir and brought the choirmaster over to push the cause. I met the minister at the door, but he didn't talk to me at coffee time. I had a good conversation with a couple of women about subsidized housing and pension plans.

The next week, another woman who remembered my name insisted on introducing me to the minister, and he recalled me from the week before. Coffee-time was old-buddy time, and the invitation was more strongly worded to come out to choir practice that week.

No one looked down on my tacky clothes or inquired too closely about my job or marital or financial status. I was a stranger, and I was welcomed.

Outward Appearance

*R*ecently I made a trip to another country, though it was located on the other side of town. I left home and lived on the amount of money I would have if I were an Old Age Pensioner, with no other means. There are all kinds of revelations, and many of them happened in flashes.

For example, I was walking back to a women's hostel where I stayed a couple of days till I found a decent room to rent. I was wearing the clothes I had borrowed from the donations room: an ugly, grey, A-line tweed skirt, a mustard-colored cotton blouse, a white acrylic sweater and a baggy, short, dull-green raincoat a couple of sizes too big for me. My hair was unkempt and growing out—both color and cut—and I had no make-up on.

I met a policeman on the sidewalk just as I was going to turn into the drive leading to the hostel. I started to nod pleasantly, as is my custom with policemen, when his cold eyes raked over me once and he nodded curtly and dismissed me.

Isn't that amazing? I thought. I am still me, inside, but no policeman has ever looked at me like that before.

Let me read you something from James 2: 8-9: "You will be doing the right thing if you obey the law of the Kingdom, which is found in the scripture, 'Love your neighbor as yourself.' But if you treat people according to their outward appearance, you are guilty of sin and the law condemns you as a law-breaker."

Do we do that? Judge people by their outward appearance? I'm afraid we do. Just let me tell you, from the other side of that judgment, from the inside looking out—I don't like it. You wouldn't either.

Who Are You?

I'm still talking about what it was like to live, as I did for a time, on the Old Age Pension. I learned a lot about survival, and about the energy it takes to survive at the bottom line. Unfortunately, energy is something old people do not have in abundance.

I reached a point where I actually thought I had a lot of money, more than enough to meet my needs, forgetting for the moment that I had no radio, no television, no newspaper, no source of entertainment other than the local library or whatever free concerts or shows that the community provides—if I had the energy to get there. Forgetting, also, that things wear out, and that in time I would have to replace sheets and towels and underwear and socks.

And when I had that flush of well-being and prosperity, I forgot for the moment my strongest desire— for a private bathroom. With my $35-a-week room, I had to share a fridge in the hall with one person and a bathroom with four men and one deaf old woman.

All this is irrelevant, really, to my main discovery. If you have put it off up till now, think about it with me. When you are alone and poverty-stricken and sitting in a room, now is the time to ponder the meaning of life and why you are here. Who are you? When you take away what you have, and what you do, who are you? Why are you here?

A Place on Earth

I've been thinking a lot about old people lately, and about their role in society.

"Old age isn't so bad," said Maurice Chevalier, "when you consider the alternative." But surely old age is a time to consider the alternative—not just cramming for exams, but putting death into its proper relationship with life. The twilight years, as someone has quaintly called them, can be a time of illumination if some serious thought goes into preparation for them.

In her book *The Second Sex*, in the section on Old Age, Simone de Beauvoir wrote this: "When [a woman] has given up the struggle against the fatality of time, another combat begins: she must maintain a place on earth."

We are all entitled to a place on earth, and it is the responsibility and duty of the younger and more fit and able in society to make a meaningful place on earth, one that is comfortable and worthwhile, for our older members. When we have done that, then we should also make it possible for them to continue to contribute to society, giving their patience and time and skill to little ones, giving their experience and memories and wisdom to the middle ones, sharing their strength and compassion with their contemporaries.

Is that too idealistic? We all know old people who are crotchety, irritable, repetitive, selfish old bores, and we prefer to stay away from them. But who and what made them that way? If we stopped to listen, they might have something to say. If we paid attention, they might stop complaining.

What Are You Doing Here?

hy are you here? I keep asking myself that. It is one of the questions that demand to be answered when one's needs are stripped to the bone and one faces reality in terms of four bare walls and subsistence-level income.

What old people have to do—and it's really what we all have to do, but with old people it is both a more apparent need and a more pressing one—what old people have to do is maintain a place on earth, and assert their right to be here. Two neat tricks when society seems to be doing its best to make you invisible.

That's what I was. I was invisible. And I wasn't even old when I went to live on the Old Age Pension, I mean, my face wasn't a sixty-five-year-old face. But I got clothes from the donations room of a local charity, and I schlepped along the streets of Toronto in them, totally invisible. Eyes of real people would flick over and past or through me in less than a twinkling.

Oddly enough, it gave me a feeling of power.

If I was invisible, I was therefore free to stare at others without their noticing me. Very freeing. Also educational. And bliss for a writer.

It's easier, I guess, for a cat to look at a king than it is for a king to look at a cat. And so I say, thanks a lot, King—the true King, Lord of us all. I know why I'm here, and God does too. That's why.

The Camel and
the Needle's Eye

*F*or some time now, I have been concerned about the plight of the aged, particularly of aging, single women. Of the poverty-stricken, better than three out of five are women, and of women over sixty-five, 44 percent are living below the poverty line.

At age sixty-five, with no other means of support, a person in Ontario can draw the Old Age Security and a Guaranteed Income Supplement from the federal government, plus a Guaranteed Annual Income Supplement from the provincial government. This comes to a yearly income which is still well below the poverty line.

Just before I went off on my project, to live on the Old Age Pension, the sermon at my church was based on the passage from Mark about the young man who came to Jesus wondering how he could assure himself of getting to Heaven. On questioning him, Jesus found that the young man obeyed all the commandments and lived an exemplary life. "Well, then," said Jesus, "sell all that thou hast and give it to the poor and follow me." And the young man went away sorrowing, for he had great wealth.

I think we are all possessed by our possessions. And the more we have, the harder it is to give them up. It was a wonderful revelation to me, how much I could live without, and the kind of freedom that gives one.

Well, I'm a camel again, looking for the eye of the needle.

How Are You Going to Blow Out All Those Candles?

You all know someone who is old, if you are not approaching old age yourself. Age, and its accompanying threats and aches and trauma, is becoming an increasing problem in our society today. It's just as well if you have some nodding acquaintance with it, before you get there yourself.

"Old age is not for sissies," said an aged aunt of mine. I have since overheard women say it to each other at the supermarket, and they didn't even know my aunt, so I guess the remark was not original to her. It's true, though, whoever said it. The aches and pains of age should be visited upon the young, who are strong enough to bear them.

On the other hand, Maurice Gaudeket, in his book *The Delights of Growing Old*, wrote: "Happiness is breathing." That's the secret, I guess, of living to be 109—just keep breathing.

I'm beginning to look forward to a spectacular old age. I will be irascible and arrogant and white-haired and eccentric and I will probably live on tea bags and toast, and I will shout at people to speak louder, and tell my children they don't visit me enough, and spoil my grandchildren rotten—God willing.

A Day In the Life

*M*aybe you know this story about the Reverend George Tuttle, past moderator of the United Church of Canada, but I just heard it. He told a friend of mine about a visit he paid to an old woman trapped by the frailties of her body in the room she lived in. Her sight was poor, too, so she had little to occupy herself with. George Tuttle asked her what she would do if she had her strength and full sight for just one day.

"Oh," she said, "for just one day!" It was a lovely game and she played it well, listing all the things she would do. Mr. Tuttle wrote down all the woman said, and then, later, he went and did all the things she had described. He wrote her a letter and told her in minute detail the events and sights and sensations of her day, thus vicariously lived, so that she was able to participate through another's experience of it.

We could do that. We all know someone old who no longer can get to the world and whom the world doesn't bother getting to. We could be someone's eyes and ears and feet for a day, or for an hour a week, on a regular basis. We could bring news and a memory of vitality to someone whose energy and strength are flagging.

I had tea every afternoon with my mother after I moved her here to live with me, and it was pleasure for *me* to describe my day to her. She didn't understand half the things I was doing—most people don't—and I found that dismaying, I must admit. But she loved hearing it all, and she approved, whatever it was. I still miss her.

Do something for someone old *now*, before it's too late.

Bears Do It

A long time ago now, over 30 years, doctors discovered that orphaned babies in institutions had a much higher mortality rate than normal, though the standards of hygiene and nutrition were adequate. The babies' unfilled need was diagnosed as anaclitic depression, caused by skin hunger. Nurses were ordered to take time to administer TLC in addition to the feeding bottle. That is, they were told to cuddle and love the babies before putting them back in their cribs. More babies survived with this treatment.

People are like that, I mean, grown-up people. We are physical human beings and we all need our quota of skin. Children need hugs for reassurance, but so do grown-ups. Older single people have a skin hunger, too, that is not easily appeased. They are often lonely and alone and have no close relatives or friends who can offer them a friendly hug.

We're all so afraid of touching. Too quickly we associate touching with some sort of sexual advance, and we shy away from it for fear of getting involved, or being misinterpreted, and we misjudge others too quickly for touching us, or for demonstrating any such physical need.

"The bad thing about getting old," one old person said to me, "is that no one ever touches you."

That's very sad, and unfortunately, very true. Old people are not only frequently trapped within four walls of a room, they are also trapped within the prison of their failing, withering bodies. No one comes near; no one touches them.

Too many friends have fallen away, either dead or too house-bound themselves to come and visit. Relatives may pay duty calls, but not often. Children and grandchildren are often thousands of miles away. Who is there to touch or hug? Those frail shoulders would square with renewed vigor if only someone could give them a pat or a hug or both.

A friend told me he hugged his mother-in-law recently and was shocked at the fragility of her body and her tiny, sharp bones, so vulnerable beneath the parchment skin. He could almost *feel* the spirit within, he said, and he was touched. *Touched.*

Touch someone old today. Give someone old a hug, and mean it. Close the generation gap with love.

Old Age is Not for Sissies

We're at that age where my friends and I are coping with aging parents. My mother died last year and my father sixteen years before that, but many of my friends' parents are still around and encountering health problems and difficulties with their living arrangements that must be common to many of you across the country. More people are living longer and the problems attendant on that fact will be increasing for the rest of this century. The population of Canada over sixty-five is increasing all the time. We are an aging society.

So, I've been thinking about old people a lot, as I see what's happening all around me. Those fortunate enough to survive into old age as couples find themselves unable to live independently, because the energy of the one isn't up to caring for the other. Flagging energy, growing frailty, failing health and dwindling financial resources are all staggering problems to the aged, as well as to their concerned children. There are no easy solutions. Trapped by failing sight or hearing and faltering legs, old people themselves feel out of step with life, and we do little for them beyond a minimum tending to their physical needs.

We keep searching for the meaning of life. Surely the wisdom and experience of old age can contribute to our understanding, if only we can cope with the physical problems and enable old people to get on with the business of living—and showing *us how*.

Consider the Lilies

y mother was never a typical grand-mother. When the children were little, she never put anything away when they came to visit, though she had a house full of precious antiques. Only once, in their collective childhood, was anything broken, and again she proved herself atypical. Liz went to her Nana with the broken object—an antique, of course.

"Oh, good!" said my mother. "That's one less thing to dust." And she really meant it. She never referred to the thing again—that's why I can't even remember what it was. I have one friend whose mother remembers not only everything the grandchildren have broken but also everything my friend and her brother broke when they were little. She keeps a running inventory. Not my mother.

Mom makes me think of Diogenes, the Greek philosopher dedicated to poverty. All he owned was the bowl in which he put the food he begged to keep himself alive. One day he stumbled and fell and broke his bowl.

"At last," he said, "I'm free!"

My mother knew all her life, it seems, that you are possessed by your possessions. Anything my mother ever owned, she owned with open hands.

And we come back to one of the paradoxes of the New Testament: it is only by letting go that you own anything.

"No man can serve two masters . . . Ye cannot serve God and mammon." God bless you, Mom, and the rest of us, too.

Love and Memory

I was talking about my mother's possessions recently, how many she had and how lightly she held them, and how towards the end of her life, she lightly dispossessed herself. She gave things away while she was still living, preferring, as she said, that people receive them from living hands rather than dead ones. She kept very little for herself, a fact that often exasperated her grandchildren and me.

We learned that she would keep very little of whatever we gave her. We began to buy gifts for Christmas, birthdays, Easter, Mother's Day and so on, on the basis of *our* liking for them, because we knew we'd get them back shortly. It became a challenge to buy her something she would actually use.

Mom gave away junk, souvenirs, old photos of the family, framed and un-, and things of real value with equal abandon. She had almost literally nothing left when she died, except her clothes, and a few precious antique cups and saucers, which I gave away. She put one lovely cup on my shelf on Valentine's Day, and it stays there.

But I found, among her few things, a collection of florists' cards bound in an elastic band. They were every card my father ever sent her, with flowers, plants or corsages, in their life together. All her Christmases, babies, anniversaries and special events were bound up in one little package of love and memory, and never thrown away.

Me? I'm a packrat. I can't bear to throw those cards away, either.

Never Mind the Chips
and Scratches

I've had this theory for years, one I call a Private History of Furniture. I bet if you look around the room you're in, or the house you're in now, you'll know what I mean. In my living room, for example, there is a round table between two chairs that my mother and her brothers and sisters gave to my grandmother for Mother's Day years and years ago. Somehow the table ended up at my parents' summer cottage, completely beat up, scratched, gouged, the finish gone.

One summer during a clean-up campaign around the cottage, I grabbed the table and sprayed it with black paint. I bought a bag of ceramic tiles and some grout and let my daughter Liz have it. She made a lovely mosaic design in blue and white and it fit nicely into the pie-crust edge of the table top. I liked it so much that when we sold the cottage and moved away, I brought the table with us.

The table is still in my living room, as I said. The tiles proved to be wonderfully impervious to stains and gouging, but the black paint is chipped now and I am reminded that the table is actually good wood—exactly what I'm not sure. One of these days, I, or someone, will go to the trouble of stripping it down and removing the tiles and restoring it to its lustrous wood finish. No reason why it can't stick around for another generation or so.

That's what I mean by a Private History of Furniture. There are things in every family that stick around. Like faith, I think. If we start with a good piece of it, there's no reason why it can't stick with us for a good long time.

I Haven't Run Out
of Pieces Yet

I'm beginning to be very grateful that I've lived as long as I have because I have so many bits and pieces squirrelled away, so many observations and anecdotes, so many things that have happened to me and my friends in the course of a lifetime that I can tell you about.

I think we do that, squirrel things away—you never know when you might need them. Few of us have the training or discipline to create a whole philosophy of life, a seamless robe that we can wear for all occasions. Instead, it looks as if we are making a patchwork quilt. We grab bits and pieces wherever we can find them, as they seem to apply to our lives, and stitch them together to make a pattern for living, something we can throw on when it gets too cold or too dark. And I'm giving you swatches of material from my work basket for you to incorporate into your design and stitch into place.

But the quilt we're making, you and I, is not really that random. It is, in fact, highly selective. It is a design for living—a Tree-of-Life pattern. It is a pattern that others wiser and more patient have developed before us.

Here's a piece I picked up that you might be able to use. A little boy I know says the opposite of backwards is goodwards. Isn't it a nice thought to face life goodwards.

Smell the Flowers While You're Here

*N*ellie McClung, who lived from 1873 to 1951, was a writer and a feminist who has only just begun to receive the posthumous attention she deserves. She had a quick wit and her pithy comments and aphorisms rate a collection in book form. I am privileged to know her niece, who *is* writing a book about her.

I first came across McClung in my grandmother's book shelves. *Flowers for the Living* was the name of the book, a collection of short stories. "Flowers for the Living" was also the name of one of the stories, about a tired cleaning woman who worked double-time to support her family. She was cleaning an office one Friday night and could not resist lying down on a couch, just for a minute. After thirty-six hours' sleep, she woke to discover that her family thought she was dead and everyone was mourning their loss of her—best mother, best cleaning lady and so on. Food and flowers had been brought to her home in abundance, and she was comforted as well as her family. She wrote the florists to thank them for *the flowers for the living*, telling them how much she enjoyed them. They ended up, if I remember correctly, using her letter as an advertising gimmick to sell more flowers, and they paid her for the idea—so you see, the story had a happy ending.

But the phrase, *flowers for the living,* became an important one in my life. To me it means that you should appreciate people while they're around—and tell them so, while they're still here. Nellie McClung should have lived so long.

Not Quite the Patience of Job, of Course

*O*h, how I wish I could always have been as patient as I am now! It would have been so much easier on my children and me. As it is, I can see the change in myself and I am grateful for it, and so are those close to me. I'll tell you how I know I've changed.

Recently, my son Matthew broke a saucer. I looked at the pieces and said, "Throw them away. We're missing a cup, anyway."

Also quite recently, Matthew knocked over a plant in the living room and there was potting soil all over the carpet. I helped him put the plant back in the pot and we vacuumed up the dirt, and I didn't shout or scream or make any disparaging remarks at all.

Finally, at last—why did it take so long?—I have realized how unimportant these minor accidents are. They simply do not matter. There are people, and I have always admired them, who have always known that, and who never seem to lose patience with their children. I was not one of them. I ranted and carried on and whipped myself to a frenzy over really trivial setbacks and minor mishaps.

And at last I have quit. I continually marvel at myself. I don't get impatient in line-ups. I don't mind a car dawdling in front of me. When I forget something and have to go back for it, I can finally say, like a woman I once knew, "If you don't use your brains, you'll have to use your legs." Isn't that amazing?

All my life I have been praying for patience. God sent me a teacher in the person of a child who needed more patience than most. It has finally paid off. For which, thanks.

Forgiveness

ave you ever forgiven anyone? Recently? How much do you know about forgiveness? It really is an incredible act, and one that only human beings are capable of—and not very often.

How *can* God forgive us? Most of the time we find it so difficult to forgive others. How in Heaven's name can He do it? Well, maybe *in Heaven's* name, we could do it, too. It all depends on love.

When my oldest daughter learned to drive, she went out on her own the day after she passed her driver's test; she drove herself to a meeting. She left early and pride prevented her from asking people to move their cars and allow her easy access out. She backed up too close to the sharp-finned fender of an adjacent car and ripped our station wagon the entire length of the right side. She drove home and burst into the house and into my arms, sobbing. I was terrified that she had hurt herself, and relieved to discover it was the car and not she who was damaged.

It *did* cost a lot to repair but he lesson I learned was worth it. I found this note in my diary from the time—and this is what I learned:

"It's not hard to forgive *totally* someone you love *totally*. Her repentance hurts me—I feel so sorry for her. So must God's love be for us—and I never understood that subjectively before."

There's No Present
Like the Time

*T*ime-management consultant Alan Lakein, who wrote the book *How to Get Control of Your Time and Your Life*, earns huge fees advising famous, busy people how to cope with the pressures of time in their lives. He says it's a question of priorities and he asks three basic questions:

1) What are your lifetime goals?

2) Where would you like to be in the next five years?

3) If you had only six months to live, and money were no object, how would you spend those months?

Does Lakein think those questions are solely for regulating your time? They sound to me as if you might actually solve all your life problems if you could answer them fully and honestly enough. They are worth thinking about.

Lakein says that once you have answered those questions, it's merely a matter of setting your priorities. You draw up your master-plan, with long-term goals and short-term goals, and then prepare specific schedules for them. Then you test the plan. Put it in your desk drawer and see if you really do what the plan says, if you really meant what you said, said what you wanted, wanted what you thought.

The best test of all is another question, according to Lakein. You're supposed to ask yourself: Am I making the best use of my time *right now*? Well—are you?

I Hope So

There is an expression in the English language that a lot of people use without knowing where it came from. Usually it is paraphrased somewhat, so that it sounds like this: "All things pass," or "It will pass," or "Other things have passed, this will too."

The original expression—and it probably wasn't original then—was first written down in an Anglo-Saxon poem called *Deor's Lament*. Anglo-Saxon poetry dates from the seventh century in England, and there is not a huge body of it extant.

It is thought that *Deor's Lament* was an even larger poem, but only a fragment of it has survived. It is an account, written in the first person, of the conflicts and sea-battles, the hardships and the deprivations the hero has suffered. He is finally alone and facing his last ordeal without any companions or support. And his constant reassuring refrain, which is repeated after each painful episode, goes like this: *thaes ofereode; thises swa maeg*.

That's the Anglo-Saxon. Here's the translation: *That passed; so may this.*

Isn't that great? I don't wish pain or hardship on anyone—they come by themselves, anyway. But isn't it *great* that we share that bleak, harsh optimism with someone who lived more than thirteen centuries ago? Somehow, it reassures me that *we* will survive.

Alone At Last

*Y*ou must have read articles about the "empty-nest" syndrome—the anxiety and emptiness that attack parents when their last child leaves home for good. Couples, they tell me, start to travel, or have the house redecorated, or take a dancng or cooking course together, and pretend they're having a second honeymoon while they try to ignore the empty space at the dining-room table, the silence in the house and the lower grocery bills.

But what about singles? As a widow, I can tell you, it's different.

My last two kids both left home last fall. Oh, the youngest one gets home from his special school most weekends, but he really is gone. I no longer have anyone to set the alarm for if I don't have an early appointment. I have to impose my own discipline. I no longer have anyone to cook dinner for every night. My grocery bills are almost zilch; my laundry is cut by two-thirds. It takes me four or five days to fill the dish-washer, so I just keep rinsing the same plate and cup. No one messes up the newspaper before I get to it. No one dirties the towels or drops crumbs on the carpet or helps me in with the groceries or chatters with me too long into the night.

Loneliness has become a habit. I have become singular, and probably too selfish, which is a danger for lonely people. For *lonely* people, not for those who are simply alone. There's a difference between being lonely and being alone, and I'm finding it out—all by myself.

Have a Nice Life

*I*t's hard for us every day, rooted as we are in reality, to keep our eyes on the infinite and our hearts set on the profundities of life. We are surrounded by bits and pieces of living every day, and we take to fussing naturally. I can't stand it if I can't eat my breakfast egg while it's piping hot, and I like the yolk to be runny, whether it's poached or boiled. I hate hard butter because it rips the toast, and the day can be ruined if the toast is too dark.

Most people are on a single-minded track when they first get up, still caught in the inner web of self and unwilling to shift into another space. They growl and grunt and adjust reluctantly to the day in uncommunicative silence.

Grudgingly, we give in to the day, open up, focus on other people and other things. It's a devastating process, one by which we drain off all the sense of our minds and the sensibility of our souls into countless irritations all day, and leave no energy for the important things. By important, I mean *human* matters. You have to take time to notice the human being who steps on your toe in the street, and the one who cuts you off in his car, and the one who elbows ahead of you in the supermarket line-up. Look at their faces. Try to understand them and why they're doing what they're doing.

Somewhere in each of us is the mystery of life. If we can learn to get through one day with each other, we come a little closer to solving it.

Swim For Your Life

I think it was Marshall McLuhan who first used the image of the goldfish in the bowl as a symbol of people in present-day society. To those who live in and of their time, as a goldfish does in its bowl, the water is invisible until there's a crack in the bowl. We are not really aware of the air we breathe, until it is cut off, nor of the society we live in, until it changes. We can't see the medium at all, though it is what we are dependent upon. McLuhan said that the artist in society is the only one who can see the water, so to speak. So it is the artist's job to describe it to us, and make us more aware of our surroundings and of the climate of thought we live in.

Of course, the artist isn't the only one who can draw our attention to our surroundings and the life we live. Jesus does a pretty good job. He made a lot of people uncomfortable when he was talking his way around Galilee, questioning the Pharisees about their motivation rather than their behavior, healing people on the no-work Sabbath, knocking over the money-changers' tables at the Temple, claimng that the Temple was, in fact, his *father's* house. He does the same for us today. His actions and challenges are just as disturbing to us now as they were when he was working his ministry, raising the dead and inactive consciences. He says terrible, hard things: give up everything you have and follow me; lose your life to find it; love your neighbor as yourself.

It hurts to think through and past our conditioning and environment. It's easier to accept the way we are as the way we should be. And then this guy comes along and makes us *think*; makes us *look* at the water we're swimming in—before it runs out.

How About Jam Today?

"Jam tomorrow, and jam yesterday—but never jam today." Remember the White Queen's explanation to Alice Through the Looking Glass, as if it were the most natural situation in the world? It is, you know. Don't you find you're *always* waiting for jam tomorrow? It seeems to me everything I'm doing or about to do depends on a decision that's going to be made tomorrow, or next week, or next month.

I entered the world of business late in life. I'm sure some of you would question whether writing is a legitimate business, but there's no disputing that I was late. So it was relatively late in my life that I discovered much of business involves waiting, simply waiting. Waiting for mail, waiting for word, waiting for a go-ahead, waiting for approval, waiting for an assignment, a contract, waiting for payment, waiting for the response. It's a wonder I haven't torn the mailperson limb from limb long before this, or ripped the phone out by its roots in my impatience to find out what's going to happen to me next.

But I have learned. I have learned what's going to happen next. *Jam tomorrow*, that's what's next. *Not* today.

How heartening, then, to listen to Jesus's words when he says, "The Kingdom of Heaven is within." That means right now, right here, you can reach out and make it yours, have it all, *today*! Heaven is a jam-today special—the love of God, and peace in your heart—all in a special package, ready for delivery now.

And isn't it a good thing, because I can't wait a minute longer!